Punch.

ALSO BY RAY MCMANUS

Red Dirt Jesus
Driving through the Country before You Are Born

Ray McManus

poems

HUB CITY PRESS
SPARTANBURG, SC

First printing, October 2014
Book Design: Meg Reid
Printed in Saline, MI
by McNaughton & Gunn Inc.
Cover Photo © Rusty Hebert

TEXT Arno Pro 10.9 / 13.1
DISPLAY Raleway

Library of Congress Cataloging-in-Publication Data
McManus, Ray, 1972-
[Poems. Selections]
Punch. / Ray McManus. pages cm
ISBN 978-1-938235-07-8 (trade paper : alk. paper)
I. Title. PS3613.C5853A6 2014
811'.6--dc23
2014034504

HUB CITY
PRESS

186 West Main St.
Spartanburg, SC 29306
1.864.577.9349

for Lindsay, Sean, Morgan, and Lennon

TABLE OF CONTENTS

GRAVEYARD

NOTES

ACKNOWLEDGEMENTS

...You've never
done something so simple, so obvious,
not because you're too young or too dumb,
not because you're jealous or even mean
or incapable of crying in
the presence of another man, no,
just because you don't know what work is.

—*Phillip Levine*

GOING IN

A dog eats its kill
from the ass first
because it's the easy
way in. At the bind,
a shift. Punch
out. The breaks
in between are never
long enough. Call it
a day anyway.

When in doubt, make
up the part in the middle.
Say it's a weak bone.
Say it's the dirt. Swallow
the voice when it rises.
And when it falls,
blame it on the dog.

FIRST SHIFT

DICK

He told me if I ever called him that
he would punch me and he told
me to get the mixing buckets
from the truck and he said be quick
and he said slow down and he told
me to watch where I stand that bulls
don't take kindly to strangers who smell
good and wear earrings and he told me
how his mother died how he didn't
cry and he asked me if I ever cried
and he called me a pussy and he told me
to get the shovel and he said he wouldn't
hold the fence forever and he said that I had
a lot to learn about work about bulls
about fences and he told me that I wouldn't
amount to much if I couldn't swing
a decent hammer and he said he wasn't
sure why the handle had a notch in it
and he asked me if I did it and he told me
to get the creosote and he told me to hold
the bucket straight and he told me to get
his water and he told me to go
sit by the tree and he told me how it was
all for shit anyway and he threw a handful
of bent nails in the air and he said it was
a shame that one day all of this would
be mine and he spit when he talked.

SATURDAY MORNINGS

To break the rabbit, hold
it by its back legs and whip it
forward. My neighbor has
names for his. He tells me
it's a myth that rabbits scream,
but I don't believe him,
and he yawns as he tosses
a wet clump of fur on the table.

Before we moved out here,
this was a prairie for the woods,
a tract for copper tubes and tin
so the wild stayed wild before
it was swallowed by cages
and cotton fields, and I
was apt to believe anything.

It's 10:00 a.m. and all the good
shows are over. Rabbits dangle
and drip on the sandy barn floor.
My neighbor tells me that
rabbits can get as big as dogs
and sometimes they eat people.

FRESHMAN

Lunch detention meant trash
pickup. There was a drainage
ditch behind the swing sets
and a zipper was stuck, so she
had to work hard to free it.
Later that day, I sat in
the principal's office, and waited
for my parents to get off work.
I was given a pencil and a sheet
of paper, told to stay quiet.
The coach in the hallway laughed.
The secretary said stop it, and
she laughed too. I heard something
about earrings and hair and I knew
it had something to do with me.
But they had the story all wrong.
I meant every word I told her.
There were no bleachers, no crowd,
no note passed in homeroom.
There was no hair either.

STAYING IN THE TRUCK

Sleight of Hand
They say Jesus could talk
from the cross because
a gypsy ran off
with the last spike.

Twist of Fate
It takes two to pick
a peach, no time
to stand there
with your mouth open.

On a Bed of Nails
I'll ring the bell.
Cut the blacktop
with kerosene.
Let me do the talking.

CLEARING HEADSTONES

On a fall afternoon, we drink Cheerwine from a glass bottle. My uncle makes a joke. I don't get it. Most of the brush has been already cleared. The game fades in and out on the truck radio. I'm 13 and I want a cigarette. We're losing.

I'm told family history with hand gestures. A great aunt died drawing water from a well. The roof fell in, she fell in, both fell in, I don't recall, only a broken neck and she was my age. I get paid when the job is finished.

The pickup sags under the weight of limbs and briars and the occasional marker. I don't think to ask. The crowd yells. I don't know who scored. My whole family is buried here. Some of the stones are rubbed out completely. One day, my uncle says, you can tell your children about this. I smile because he's nice, but I have no idea what he's talking about, or if he's even talking to me.

It's the fourth quarter. A breeze blows. I think we're done for now. My uncle meets me behind the truck—we did good work today. I don't know how to whistle. I want to leave and never come back. I want to know who'll win the game, but I know so little, just what's heavy, the body's protests, splinters beneath the skin.

BREAK

Every pine tree has my face on it. I am somewhere between not being a tow truck or a beard. I am not molasses or lima beans or split-rail fences around barns. I carry a bark. I carry a scar on my left knee. This is how I grow up despite most of the curses mumbled before I got here: chicken houses, junk yards, wild dogs. I am not cornbread or copper wiring. I am not the story of every kid who punched back the dust, pulled up election signs, and threw bricks through school windows. I am not the story of every broken bottle on the straw. I am the straw.

DISTURBING REMAINS

The easiest way to put a truck in
a ditch is to ignore broken fences.

Sometimes the crash is on purpose,
and we bury the headstone.

The older the stone, the better
the chances, ask the field about shatter.

Ask a salesman about hosepipes.
Ask Sid about the bottom of his boot.

These are the things we eat to remember,
our dust-mouth, the pig in us, rooting.

TESTIMONY

We were lost, hungry, and hopeless, creeping toward the pipelines in a '78 Buick Regal with Big Star on the radio, and Todd had salvation in his pocket, just no way to bring it, and there was panic until we found a bible and thumbed our way toward a middle passage and tore a page out. We rolled with it, and the glory of it shined against the dashboard, and for every word that could've been spoken there could've only been one way to say it when the cloud broke for the opened window. Amen.

SOMEWHERE IN THE MIDDLE

Houses are set in rows
like teeth with yellowed
veneers and the men
wake up to clean their yards
while their wives peer
through bent slats in blinds
to make sure they stay
on task. And they never do.

It's hard not to stare at people
who don't live here, their
young fingers tapping on
the dash as they pass through
to turn around, but the men
know that the best way
to avoid seeing dead birds
in a nest is by ignoring them.

Behind the neighborhood,
trees push back the constant
hum of cicadas and mowers,
and the men recognize the tune
as the song they've heard
since birth, their bodies
brown from the sun, bent
forward, not listening.

AN OFFERING

Whatsoever thy hand findeth to do, do it with thy might; for there is no work
—Ecclesiastes 9:10

A blurred church.
A boy in the middle
of a half-finished foyer.

Plaster falls in slow
motion like ash
over rebar crosses.

Boot. Wall. Fist.
Boot. Wall. Fist.
Boot. Wall. Fist.

Dust falls over
the open door,
a silhouette.

The sound of feet
dragging in the dark.

ON THE TOUR AT DJJ

They gather halos from the field and drown them in buckets under the tap. The deputy gets loud, and busted vandals start to sing. When he laughs, imagine lines and about-faces, buckles, and not bending. Think about hair pulling and the motor coughing to start, the way you must look when you realize the road doesn't dead end after all. For every time the deputy rakes the stick across the bars, think a love poem tattooed on the gums, the iron on the anvil. For every shove against the wall, think a fall afternoon on your parent's back porch, the air cool against a hot sun, birthdays, sex, the sleep you had before the dog went missing. Then when the deputy looks you in the eye, he'll stop laughing.

PIPELINE

The car idles fast. The last one was totaled.
At the crossroads, teeth are thrown and go missing.
We keep our love in pillowcases and bang them on banks
when the radio plays sad songs because there's nothing

else to do. Out here nobody cares to see where bones
land, because this is the place to lose things, where rust
sleeps in pastures, where horses go to die. According
to the map, the route of egress stops somewhere

between backfill and setback, so we crash on the edge,
half in/half out, split by hard-cut and easement,
the product of not paying attention to the length
of ditches. And like the afternoons of so many

wasted days and all that is half buried, this is nothing
new, just a cut of it, the mess we leave behind.

MINIMUM WAGE

I want to hold money
in my hand, fold it over
and put it in my pocket.
I want to hold money
in my hand and put it in
the dresser drawer
and forget about it.
I want to hold money
in my hand and walk
into a department store
and say this is for you,
and this is for you,
and this is for you.

I want to smell money
in my hand. I want
the smell money leaves
on my hand, your hands.

I want to smell the blush
on your face when I take
what's folded in my pocket
and lay it out on the bed
before you.

I don't care how much it costs.

PUNCH IN

It's called probation
because you can go
at any minute and
it's stupid to believe
in heaven. Dick gives
a shove, and you
stab the floor where it
meets the wall and rake
over the tackless strip
with the stair tool.
He takes it from you
and shows you the proper
way. Again. And you need to
understand backing,
what breaks under weight
and angle. The phrase
is break then rake.
And soon Guy tells you
to get the tools together
and load up the van.
Later he tells which
carpet lays best, seam
and pile, padding and density.
He never asks you about
your parents, or where you
went to school. He doesn't
ask if you brought money
for lunch. He doesn't ask
if you have a ride home either.

RECEIVING

After pulling pallets, you don't mind slinging a few cases of lunchmeat over the counter—especially if you're still high from break. You've been trained to pull dates, to rotate, to look past head cheese, to let the cooling fans drown out the soft-spoken customers digging through the packages for discounts. Occasionally you will be touched—the seafood clerks speaking to themselves in third person, halibut slapping parchment, the urge to sample. Sometimes, you will be approached by the same half-naked woman who'll take anything but a hint. And you'll act like the assistant manager who only makes important decisions, offer two for one on the split packs where the gel has yet to seep. You have authority: two weeks of training, a closing banquet, a handshake, and a plaque. Service is the price you pay for air conditioning. Sometimes, a woman with bad makeup and saggy tits is easy to talk to. And when your manager calls for baggers on the intercom, and the bell rings at the loading dock, the woman is still standing there; you tell her you'll be right back. Sometimes, there are worse things than lying.

SMALL ENGINE REPAIR

Jeff stands, feet spread and back straight, and I listen to him tell the customer that I'm new here. The customer nods to the mower on the sidewalk. I get it. A good mechanic is drawn to an engine. A good mechanic is part chassis and crank, oil and water. But a small engine mechanic hovers and grunts, finds a way, uses pliers on rusted bolts. You borrow tools and work under the outside lean-to, not near Rush and his Camaro Jacket, not at the shop table near the fan and radio.

We haven't seen our boss in days. Jeff takes a twenty from the cash box, tells me to get him a biscuit and to bring back the change. I imagine what his trailer looks like, how it could be possible for him to have sex with his wife when she's awake. I think about quitting and taking the money. Sunlight reflects off the showcase chrome. His hand is out. He never says thank you.

The power stroke: just before the piston and crankshaft reach top dead center, a spark. Take what fuels us, the air we breathe and smash them together: the boss on vacation, Jeff manning the counter, Rush pouring gasoline.

Everything that has been taken in and thrown back is tossed aside just as quickly, unlike the two stroke principle and all of its scavenging. I'm better for it: the blow-down, the displacement, the wrench in my hand, Jeff facing the opposite direction.

THE BLACKSMITH

Blistered hands, hearts, and tongues, give
way to callus, the need to alter, to repair,
to thicken—this is patience. There isn't
a track for the haunted to follow, to go
from forge to pound, to collar, to grind,
to strain silent, slow, and solemn, only iron
stress and the fire that saves the bowed
from broken. The beating makes what was
strong stronger, but I am no more iron,
or the slip-choke of fire stoked and running
too hot—this is temper and upset,
control and measure. A hammer holds
the bitter back. What flies, what's fatal,
what sprawls or shrivels, no matter
the motion, no matter the difference,
what sends each strike a promise that a day
is just another piece to shoulder, another
way for drawing out, another way
for the soul to drift, what refuses
to die, what gets taken to the cusp will be
better than it was before—this is the saving
of ruin. To quench. To blacken. To harden.

SWING SHIFT

HOW TO ADD A PORCH TO A TRAILER

Christmas Eve, 1987, blown
in an F-150, and no one told you
that this is about as good
as you're going to get.
With your right hand pushing
against the passenger headrest,
your left a vice grip on the wheel,
you still think the best is yet to come.
And even though you met her
in a parking lot, you think
you'll get married anyway,
start your own hauling company,
have kids, dogs, why not?
What are the chances
that the second kid will come
with complications, that his mother
will never heal right,
or that you'll be cleaning shit
for years? Addition is easy.

ROOKIE MISTAKE

Sit on the tongue
of a trailer for hours
stuck between a field
and a two-lane, a blowout,
and the weight of it.

It will take hours to fix this.

Listen to the men
challenge the obvious—
this is the middle
of nowhere, you weren't
in her house long enough
to do anything. Butt in.
Accept that this is your
fault. Argue with them.
Show them your move
before you throw
the first punch.

JAWBONE

As if Charles Napier still spoke
in Kentucky, I'll tell you what I know
about pine trees: Bark. Sap. Needles.
Cones. They smile with no teeth.

Unless they threaten a dwelling
or utility or obstruct the construction
of said dwelling and/or utility, unless
they are dead or dying, there is no real

reason to cut them down. They're a soft
wood, weakened with age much
like human jawbones, only they do less
damage when they fall. From top

to bottom they are more flexible.
Good for pulp. Shit for firewood.

DROPPING THE TREE WHOLE

It's called throw and go,
and I fall asleep.
We are there in no time.
I get the ropes, the spikes,
and Dean makes a dick joke about Clinton,
and it's just a matter of time
before he will ask who I voted for.
I'll say I don't.
He'll say good.
And we'll move on.

To disconnect a chain link fence,
find the weakest point at the gate.
Roll.

SPUR CLIMBING

Push. Stab. Hump. Rest.
They call it dying to get
to heaven, and half way
up the tree you'll stop.
And while the saw slaps
the trunk, Dean will stand
on the ground and yell
for you to keep going.
But your right knee will
lock, and the rigging will
cut into your inner thighs.
This is not the place for love.

You will guess the distance
you have left. You will get
it wrong. Push off your
strong foot; stab with
the other. Hump
the tree easy. The rest
is in the harness. Look
to the tree for forgiveness.
Its arms like limbs will be
outstretched, waiting.
They will say *hold me*.

ABDUCTION

After demonstrating
how to remove pine
sap with gasoline,
today's lesson
is about girls.
Dean leans
against the chipper
truck and tells me
he can get any girl
to walk over,
and *look at me,*
he says. And I do.
His hair knotted
on his shoulders,
his seed cap pulled
down to just above
his eyes. *There's one.*
I try to disguise
my embarrassment.
I know how I smell.
The gasoline still
strong on my chest.

And she's smoking.

CLEARING BRUSH OFF THE ROOF

I ask the sun to be jealous when they yell
hurry up. I wonder if the ground ever forgives.
Don't mind me, I'd say, *I'm just passing through*.
But I wish I could stay. I like it here—just me,
the sun, and the ghosts I've kept—but this job
requires too much balance, the ability to counter
slope and tongue, and the house below me
is empty. Not even looking hard, and I've
already seen more than I knew before I climbed
up here. I don't know the difference between
peak and valley, just ground and sky, and
occasionally, days like this, when I am neither.

ABOUT THAT BREAK, DEAN: IT WAS NOTHING.

Rain slack.
Off soon.
Dents in
the yard,
full.

Stumps stand
like pitchers
throwing
in the outfield.

The tree closed
its eyes,
so we ate
it. Dark
by field,
light
behind it.

Sky?
Hard to say.
Not sure
which way
the wind
is blowing.

NOSEBAG

for Sean Thomas Dougherty

The back end
of any limb
will break,
kick-back.

Back up.

The boss
runs the truck.
The boss
breaks the rake.

Be the rake.
Dig. Punch. Jam.
Use a stick, not your hands.

Plastic against
metal don't
sound like wood
against metal,
don't sound
like sand
against metal,
you should
know this,
but you don't
see how,
and you don't
see the boss's
lunchbox either.

Summer's blood
beats beneath
the skin.

Don't bend.

The chipper
whines, hums
its rebel song.

You feed; it eats.
Mouth is tongue,
tongue is throat.
More throttle,
less choke.

Teeth stay fixed
in constant revolution.

FOR THE MIDDLE-AGED HOUSEWIFE WATCHING ME RAKE HER YARD

Set your porch on fire
and invite me in.
I won't mind
if you call me boy
or ask me what I think
about the heat
as if I could do anything
about it, as if I wanted to.
I won't mind your paper-
back love, if that is
what you want to offer.
It will burn all the same.

WAITING ROOM

My boot fills with blood.
My knee is sliced open
and packed with sawdust,
and I am eager to know
what I will get. *Keep it
elevated*, they said, *until
the nurse calls you*. Heavy
breathers will watch
whatever is placed in front
of them. On the television
there is a show about kidney
stones and I shift in my seat
to get a better look. All these
open mouths giving me
a glimpse of what we look like
on the inside without bones.

DOG BOX

I. Drip Line

I can tell when it's lunch
by squinting at the sun
and standing against the base
of a tree with an ax in my hand.
The foreman yells shave it.

This time I won't fall in love
with the sound bark makes
as it flips in chunks
across the lawn. I won't pay
attention to sap or sand or imagine
I'm in the top of the tree
screaming that I'll jump
if I have to. This time I'll get
lucky and won't stand in a bed
of ants or a nest of yellow jackets,
won't hear what sloshes in the tank,
won't feel the saw on my knee.

II. *Dicking Around*

The foreman will lean in to say
the numbers like it was bad
news about his mother.
He will look both ways first,
never lifting his eyes. I like that.

When the truck is full, someone
has to dump it, someone has to
stay. I imagine someday us going
together, doesn't matter
who's driving, and when static
settles on the radio and whatever
song begins to play, he'll say
what he always says—you know
all songs are really about fucking.

We keep the ropes in the dog
box, all the rigging, and mixed
tools. The foreman tells me to
learn the names, but if I ask,
he yells at the weather as if
he always wants it to rain,
and I'll know not to ask why
because I like being up front.
So I take a rake and lean on it.

III. *Worker's Compensation*

Lunch won't be here
for another hour,
so when the rain
comes it is welcomed
and we sit on empty
buckets under a tin
overhang with our boots
soaked and watch
the bull-rope take water.
I can count the stitches
from the inside of my knee
by the pull. My luck
is measured in metric,
fraction, and the will
to prop. The guys talk
about bow-saws and cant
hooks, broken chains across
the face, pinions stripped
and toes missing. They
tell me I'm lucky
and point to the rope.

IV. *Busted Out*

When the hitch breaks
and the trailer sags, we weld
it back where we can,
and the foreman yells
flash burn and tells me
not to stare at the arc,
and of course I try
to see how long I can
stare without blinking
for Darvocet, for blisters,
for an early trip home,
but I'm not going anywhere,
not with these kinds of promises.

So bad eye closed, mouth shut,
and no muscle I learn
the difference between friction
and tension, the hold that slips
when the tree comes down.
At the stump, the foreman
yells shave it, and this time
I won't fall in love
with the sound of grunt
and grind, the leaf in the wind
before the skin hits the chipper.

V. *Bone Pile*

The truth never hurts
when there is love,
but there is no love here,
no way to look at what
happened as an accident.

New guys ride in the box.
New guys who cut themselves
with chainsaws ride in the box
alone. The foreman says
it's because I'm cursed,
but I'm not convinced
he understands curses.

I rest my knee over a pile
of wet rope with my back
to the open window and let
the pills work. I close my eyes
to a highway humming over
sirens punctuated by pot-holes
and Jake Brakes. Sometimes
I hear laughter from the cab.
I wonder what they have
to talk about, where they get
the heel to laugh at miss-cuts
as part of the initiation.
But in a few minutes I won't
care. I'm already starting to feel
nothing—such a small blessing.

GRAVEYARD

PUNCH

a.
The business model: violent loneliness,
always an office down the hall. Place
desk to face the door. Avoid windows.

b.
Shit flows downhill.

c.
The memo: top-heavy. Weak support.
You are a bill on the counter marked
late. Do not telegraph your move.

d.
When a blow strikes you directly in the head
the front of your cranium is forced back into
the frontal lobes of your brain. Read that shit
again. The front of your cranium is forced back
into the frontal lobes of your brain.

e.
Ask the stick what it thinks about flexing
before it breaks, but call it a pencil.

f.
Angles are no good. You give up too much.
The chin, the jaw, the flat bridge of the nose:
all strong openers against distracting presentations.
A hit directly to the face, despite the slideshow,
is an ideal situation. Note to self:
it's called follow through.

g.
Like eating spoiled food, it has to come out –
the actor yelling and slamming doors in the break
room. This is the business end, point it toward
the end of the barrel. Sleep while they work.
This is how you make something of yourself.

GENERAL

By Tuesday afternoon
the voices in the hall
have melted into one.
I try to muscle up
the courage to peel
off my face and eat it,
but I can't, too weak,
I say, and stay bent over
the edge and bite the desk
instead. Each cubicle folds
into the next until I rise,
and it's Friday, and no one
has the guts to speak
of overtime. I count
the steps twice and brush
by papers on the bulletin
board. They stand at
attention and salute me
one after another as they
should. As they should.

ORDER OF OPERATIONS

The story is the same.
A dead end where it begins,
already dying. A cigarette
burning in the break room
ash tray, lighting another
one. Dying to forget.

Horses forget nothing.
They remember faces,
hands, don't care much
for riding, but do it
anyway. And they die
in their sleep standing up.

In your stall, you take
the script, pick up
the phone. The lines
are written for you.
Skip the parts
you're dying to leave.
The good parts.

PERFORMANCE EVALUATION

To fly, one needs to conquer
the force of weight,
one needs lift. That's what
wings are for.
      To produce lift,
one needs propulsion.
That's what engines are for.

To keep moving, one simply
needs to cut back the drag.
That's what you are for.

PUNCHING ABOVE YOUR WEIGHT

It's hard not to notice
what you want to see
like the possum
when it assumes
the tired position.
Smile;
play dead.

You claim
you understand
a dead language,
that you know
the difference
between a soft
and pitiless gaze.
But that's just you:
curled
with your nose
down, eyes glazed,
dead set
on pretending.

DRY

A conference full of men and women trying
too hard to arrange the seating when really
they should just fuck and get it over with.

Nylon over knees, eyes that stretch across
and always downward, awkward chuckles,
the fumble for loose change, the constant

fingering of the collar, and his name is always
Steve and her name is always forgotten.
The morning sessions come and go, blue suit,

black suit, tight skirts and blouses, a desert
of V-necks and coffee cups, khakis crashing
into the dust that flutters in the fluorescent.

This is the power of makeup. Note the envy
that comes in sizes, the smile that's nature's way
of saying *I'm sorry, can I put my fingers in your mouth?*

BEING THE ONLY SMOKER AT THE CONFERENCE

The desert is a great
place to hear a voice,
especially hers.
So he puts his tongue
in the sand and whispers—
is this what you meant?

And if the sky has
an answer it will call out—
it could be.

THE EXTRAORDINARY DREAM OF AN ORDINARY PERSON

We walk the field and pull halos
from the rain and smash them
with a mallet. You say we'll be
together forever, and we leave
the pieces where they lay. Weeks
from now we'll come back here,
but give it months, maybe years,
and eventually I'll get scared
that we've lost the way. I'm not
thinking about that now. I let
the rain rob me blind and follow
you because we're in this much
together and there's thunder,
and somewhere between this row
and the one farthest from where
we started, I dropped the mallet.
I'm all backwards, turned around.
I panic when I can't see you bent
behind a basket full of halos
I've never seen before. Do you love
me? Tell yourself you love me.

ULCERS

For all the borrowed
tools I've broken.

For all the lip
and fear and hope.

For all the nights
I curse the mistakes
I've already forgotten.

For sparks that spray
from the grinder.

For the way she smells
when I find her.

For the times I don't
think to bother.

APPRAISAL

There's a desk between us—
might as well be the Grand
Canyon, and I might as well
be a tourist with a broken
translator and a car in the ditch.
The story is one that gets told
as it happens: the boy
on the sidewalk cries, his ball
flattened in the road. It's
a common theme, but in this
story the driver accelerates
and swerves on purpose,
and no matter how much
that boy wants to grow up
and punch the driver in the face,
she gets away with it.

HUNGER

That hole,
that mouth,
that hollow road,
that mound of dirt,
that swallow
that hangs
from trees,
that push
that's always
down,
that's nothing,
says the ground.

Shhh,
says the ocean.

WHEN YOU GOT NOTHING COMING

Standing in line at the Quick Way, behind the guys from S&T construction, I think about the relief we get from clearing. A boy behind me came in with them, mud falling off his boots. I want to loosen my tie and tell him how much I miss it.

I buy two magazines because I don't know when I'll go home, drink Coors, and pretend that life is good for non-smokers. Sometimes I can't keep my good eye on the dead, take a long walk in the yard, and look for a hole to fall in. Sometimes I play old country songs and imagine I'm in prison. Sometimes it's for real. To take what's coming through the bean slot. To begin every letter never sent the same way. To be locked up for as long as I can remember.

WHAT IS NOT HARASSMENT?

We've become a Race of Peeping Toms
Reader's Digest, April 1939.

Call me Jeff and ignore me
in the back room where my
desk is, the rear window.

So much care is given up front.

The grounds crew works
to free the drainage back-up
in the parking lot below.

Occasionally they look up.

Ask me what it's like to open
your eyes in dirty water, to
refuse to feed from the bottom.

Ask me about pension.

Ask me about the flood out
back, how to spit out the hard
pieces stuck in the throat.

My wet skin, the blinds open.

AT THE LAST REUNION

This is
Charlie Daniels.

This is
fire on the mountain.

This is
a jar emptied
as our stomachs
on the sand.

This is
the ghost
of a pipeline,
the rust
on the fan.

This is Todd
on the hood
of my car.

He's dead now.

RANSOM

When I asked you for a ride,
I wanted you to tell me to get in
the trunk. I would've lived there
for days with old bread the size of love,
and a lug wrench. I could tell you why
my teeth are loose, why my thumb pops
when I move it, how stairs are no longer
an option because of my knee. I could
sing you a theme song for a desert at dawn,
and, in the heat of day, drip through a hole
and become the rust you are looking for.
Did you know that stars only look brilliant
because we tell them to? That clouds are
the sky's way of hiding the shame of its accent?
Did you know that when I was fifteen
I stole a car, wrecked it, and parked it
in my neighbor's driveway because
we wanted to go to the mall to steal
t-shirts and watch Erik break Milli Vanilli
records because shitty records deserve
to be broken? I could be a broken record—
a snap and a stain. I'm not afraid of the dark.

PUNCHING OUT

We'll go out of this world
the same way we came,
same pull, same fight,
different door. Blindfolded
and carried out, left
with only the maps of day
and breaks cut into our faces.
Some of us will reach out
stranded for a home
we've never seen, and learn
to crash against the sky
rather than dig at brick.
The rest will push our heads
against the freezing dark
behind us, hoping to break
back in line, to fall through
the dream of flight, begin
the decent, still-born again.

OUR DAILY BREAD

Every day is 4 a.m. Every day is wet autumn. Every day is a man dying alone in his kitchen. Every day is a dog named Biscuit. Every day is spit on the carpet. Every day is the bottom of a bucket. Every day is slide guitar.

Every day is dirt slung out in the garden. Every day is a mountain punching the sun. Every day is a cut-out cowboy. Every day is a cardboard dream.

Every day is caught somewhere between the blather and noise of exploding faces. Every day is an eye torn open. Every day is a gate rusted stuck. Every day is a spur dragging in the dirt. Every day is a broken boy.

Every day is a busted throat. Every day is dry swallow. Every day is Vicodin and tumbleweed.

Every day is an open mouth choking on painted paper. Every day is a trailer and a cactus. Every day is a note asking for something back. Every day is rapture. Every day is cartoon complete.

WHEN WE STOPPED TALKING ABOUT THE WEATHER

Language itself is just dust, crystalline particles, a blue snow descending
in silence.
　　　　　　—Campbell McGrath

This country life has a limited vocabulary—
call it rural, full of foul language,
tracks dug in with more fences to ride,
more horses to break. It's full of itself.
When you were wild, you learned real fast
that the secret to being a pony is survival;
you believed the rope was a miracle,
and learning to let go was just
enough to discover God. But no matter how
much you want to climb, the dust
and sage and granite won't let you go there—
no God, no heaven dotted in crystalline
patterns, just heat and sand gone too far.
This place won't die easy, only in bits,
in particles, in stories braided in tongue.
The forest becomes a field, the field
becomes a plot, a fire, an escape, a chimney
left standing, a finger poking a hole in a blue
sky, then rain. It is the myth of dreams—
flooded pastures will never fill with snow.
It is the dirt road, its path rutted and forever.
It is the frontier descending into pine
and sparkleberry, fractured in the fall.
It is the suit you'll be buried in—a thicket,
a briar song, a mouth of honey and dirt,
a drift, a rattle, the damp silence.

NOTES

"Going In:" Whereas I cannot confirm that dogs eat their kill from the ass first through scientific research, I have seen it happen on two separate occasions. Both times, it made sense.

"Staying in the Truck"—the italics are from the song "With or With You" written and performed by U2. Kerosene is used for asphalt sealer when black-topping driveways.

"On the Tour at DJJ"—DJJ, the South Carolina Department of Juvenile Justice.

"Nosebag"—another word for lunchbox. Also the bag they hang from a horse's nose. Same thing. For Sean Thomas Dougherty—a good friend who eats his lunch in the Rust Belt, and one of the few remaining true revolutionaries of the working class. "The Asplundh Whisper Chipper with a Ford 4 cylinder gas engine can run as high as 3500 RPM and eat through a pine tree as big as round as your head. Speaking of your head, it will eat that too."—advice from my foreman on my first day with the tree service. "Nosebag" was originally published as "Rake/Chip/Spoon," *Pea River Review*.

"Dog Box"—A separate enclosed area on a work truck that sits between the cab and rear assembly, commonly known as "the back." Some are equipped with a bench seat; others are simply used for storage. They all have poor ventilation, and absolutely zero safety features. Cabs were redesigned to fit larger crew sizes in the front of the vehicle, and dog boxes for human passengers are no longer manufactured today. Sadly, they no longer manufacture Darvocet either.

"Punch."—The quote "When a blow strikes you directly in the head the front of your cranium is forced back into the frontal lobes of your brain. Read that shit again. The front of your cranium is forced back into the frontal lobes of your brain" was taken from a blogpost titled WHAT EXACTLY HAPPENS WHEN YOU GET PUNCHED IN THE FACE?

"What is not Harassment?"—The quote is from Hitchcock's classic *Rearwindow*:

> Stella: We've become a race of Peeping Toms. What people ought to do is get outside their own houses and look in for a change. Yes sir. How's that for a bit of homespun philosophy?
>
> Jeff: Readers Digest, April 1939.

"Our Daily Bread"—originally published as "American Poem #2" in *Pea River Review*.

AKNOWLEDGEMENTS

A deep appreciation to the editors of these journals, sites, and anthologies who published these poems:

Barley South Review: "Freshman" originally published as "Sixth Grade" and "The Extraordinary Dream of an Ordinary Person" originally published as "American Poem #4"

Pea River Review: "Nosebag" originally published as "Rake/Chip/Spoon," and "Our Daily Bread" originally published as "American Poem #2"

moonShine Review: "Receiving"

The Pinch: "Dick" and "General"

Animal: "Saturday Mornings"

Frank Martin Review: "Waiting Room" and "For the middle-aged housewife watching me rake her yard"

Steel Toe Review: "An Offering"

Blue Collar Review: "Punching Out"

Remaking Moby: "The Blacksmith"

Hayden's Ferry Review: "Clearing Headstones"

Town Creek Poetry: "Minimum Wage"

Jasper Magazine: "At the Last Reunion"

A Sense of the Midlands Anthology: "Saturday Mornings" and "When we stopped talking about the weather"

Found Anew Anthology: "Pipeline"

Grit Po: Rough South Poetry Anthology: "Dog Box," "Disturbing Remains," and "Staying in the Truck"

Much appreciation is given to my mentors Kwame Dawes and Ed Madden, and my wife Lindsay—my first reader always. Without them this book could not be possible. Thank you to my dad and Mr. Green for the hand and the heart. Also a special thank you is given to the University of South Carolina's Office of the Provost whose generous Creative and Performing Arts Grant gave me the time to write.

HUB CITY
PRESS

HUB CITY PRESS is a non-profit independent press in Spartanburg, SC that publishes well-crafted, high-quality works by new and established authors, with an emphasis on the Southern experience. We are committed to high-caliber novels, short stories, poetry, plays, memoir, and works emphasizing regional culture and history. We are particularly interested in books with a strong sense of place.

Hub City Press is an imprint of the non-profit Hub City Writers Project, founded in 1995 to foster a sense of community through the literary arts. Our metaphor of organization purposely looks backward to the nineteenth century when Spartanburg was known as the "hub city," a place where railroads converged and departed.

HUB CITY PRESS poetry

Pantry • Lilah Hegnauer

Waking • Ron Rash

Eureka Mill • Ron Rash

Checking Out • Tim Peeler

Twenty • Kwame Dawes, editor

Home Is Where • Kwame Dawes, editor

Still Home • Rachel Harkai, editor

Voodoo For the Other Woman • Angela Kelly